Serving from the Heart
Finding Your Gifts and Talents for Service
Leader Guide

Serving
from the Heart

Finding Your Gifts and Talents for Service

LEADER GUIDE

Carol Cartmill & Yvonne Gentile

ABINGDON PRESS
Nashville

SERVING FROM THE HEART:
FINDING YOUR GIFTS AND TALENTS FOR SERVICE
LEADER GUIDE

Copyright © 2011 by Abingdon Press

This book is printed on acid-free paper.

ISBN 978-1-426-73600-1

11 12 13 14 15 16 17 18 19 20—10 09 08 07 06 05 04 03 02 01

MANUFACTURED IN THE UNITED STATES OF AMERICA

CONTENTS

FOREWORD

I have an old toolbox that belonged to my great grandfather, Joseph Lorson. He was a carpenter who built homes in Kansas City in the early 1900s. Inside are a myriad of antique tools. Some of the tools I recognize. Others are more mysterious to me; I am not sure how they were used or what purpose they served.

As I look through his box, I am surprised by what seems to be a duplication of tools. There are a half dozen saws—each having a different size or cutting blade. There are different kinds and shapes of chisels and planes. I would love to know when my great grandfather used a particular tool as opposed to another one.

I have debated about what to do with these tools. My father passed them on to me as a gift—a legacy. Should I mount them on a special wall as a tribute to my family heritage? Perhaps I should carefully preserve them in their box and pass them on to my children. Because I am uncertain about what to do with them, they sit in their wooden toolbox in one corner of my garage.

But every once in awhile I have a need for one of these tools—usually a saw, but sometimes a chisel or a hammer. So I take one of the tools from the box and put it to use. Instantly there is a sense of satisfaction as the tool does exactly what it was made to do. These tools were meant to be used! They were designed to build things!

I also have come to appreciate the nuances between some of the tools. The small, thin blade of the trim saw was perfect when I needed to replace a piece of molding in my study. But the large handsaw did the trick when branches were broken and hanging from my trees after an ice storm.

Of course, the metaphors are apparent. Each of us has been given gifts by the Holy Spirit—spiritual tools. Some of the gifts are mysterious; we are not sure how they work or what purpose they serve. Others are readily identified and easy to use. But all are meant to be used—not safely hidden away.

What is more, when we understand which spiritual gifts may be needed for a particular kind of task in the church, help persons identify their spiritual gifts, and then align the right people for the right tasks, the work of the ministry is more effective and the experience of those doing the ministry is full of joy—for they have found the very thing they were gifted to do. It is amazing the difference the right tool can make when approaching a difficult task.

Carol Cartmill and Yvonne Gentile have done a remarkable job of helping hundreds of people discover their spiritual gifts and to begin using them within the church. As a result of their efforts, the people of our church are more effectively serving God, the ministry is growing and expanding, and our members are discovering joy, not drudgery, in their ministry for Christ.

This program is an excellent guide to discovering and making the most of the tools that the Holy Spirit places in our toolboxes.

Adam Hamilton
Senior Pastor
The United Methodist Church of the Resurrection

Teaching
Serving from the Heart

Welcome to *Serving from the Heart: Finding Your Gifts and Talents for Service*. You have a variety of tools to choose from as you prepare to lead your group. The Leader Kit includes this leader guide and a DVD.

There are seven session plans in the leader guide (Sessions 1-6 are required; "Putting It All Together" is recommended but optional). Each session plan includes the following:

- The objective for the session
- Instructions for preparing for the session
- A list of materials needed
- A welcome
- Suggestions for prayer
- Helps for leading the session, including two video segments (see DVD contents below)
- Group and individual activities with step-by-step instructions and suggested time allotments for completing each activity

The DVD includes the following:

- Two video segments for each session—one with leader tips and helps to use in preparing and conducting your group study, and a teaching segment to play during class time
- Seven sets (one set per session) of overhead slides to print onto transparencies or project on a wall or screen (These are optional but may be especially helpful with large groups of twenty or more people.)
- A digital photo slide show for use (either printed or projected) in Session 5 on Dreams
- A print copy of the Spiritual Gifts Discovery Tool

- Forms and handouts for use in class, including:
  - ◦ Biblical Foundation Chart
  - ◦ Blank handouts for the Tapestry of My Life Exercise
  - ◦ Ministry Matching Exercise
  - ◦ S.T.R.I.D.E. Ministry Profile forms

We encourage you to become familiar with the material here, including the extra (optional) resources, and customize your teaching plan to fit your unique audience and setting.

Class Sessions: Format Options

Serving from the Heart can be taught in six or seven 45- to 60-minute sessions, or in four 2-hour sessions, or as a weekend retreat. The following outline may help you plan your sessions.

45- to 60-minute format	2-hour format	Weekend Retreat
Session 1: Spiritual Gifts: Biblical Foundation *Participant Chapter 1*	**Session 1:** Spiritual Gifts: Biblical Foundation *Participant Chapter 1* *Spiritual Gifts Discovery Tool* *(No Participant Chapter)*	**Morning Session:** Spiritual Gifts, Talents & Resources *Participant Chapters 1-3* *Spiritual Gifts Discovery Tool* *(No Participant Chapter)*
Session 2: Spiritual Gifts Defined *Participant Chapter 2*	**Session 2:** Spiritual Gifts Defined *Participant Chapter 2* **Session 3:** Talents and Resources *Participant Chapter 3*	**Afternoon Session:** Individuality, Dreams, Experiences *Participant Chapters 4-6* and Putting It All Together
Session 3: Talents and Resources *Participant Chapter 3*	**Session 4:** Individuality *Participant Chapter 4* **Session 5:** Dreams *Participant Chapter 5*	
Session 4: Individuality *Participant Chapter 4*	**Session 6:** Experiences *Participant Chapter 6* **Putting It All Together** *Participant Putting It All Together*	
Session 5: Dreams *Participant Chapter 5*		
Session 6: Experiences *Participant Chapter 6*		
Putting It All Together and Making a Connection *(Recommended but Optional Session)*		

Session 1
Introduction and Biblical Foundation

Objective for This Session:
To gain a biblical foundation for understanding spiritual gifts.

Preparation: Read in advance Before You Begin and Chapter 1 in the workbook, and Session 1 in the leader guide. Read all Bible passages. Try all instructions given both in the workbook and the in the leader guide.

Watch the leader tips and classroom DVD video segments, "Introduction and Biblical Foundation." As you prepare for the session, you might also enjoy watching the video "Putting It All Together" for an overview of the class and its benefits. If you are using overhead slides, either print the overheads for Session 1 for use on a projector or bring the disk to use with a computer and projector.

Materials Needed: blank nametags; pens or pencils; white board or flipchart with appropriate markers; participant workbooks

Welcome and Introductions (5 minutes)

As participants arrive, hand them their workbooks and ask them to make nametags for themselves.

Welcome everyone to *Serving from the Heart*. Explain that it is a six-week continuing course with a recommended but optional concluding session (or a four-week course if you have chosen to combine sessions into two-hour segments). Let them know that, at the end of the course, they will have learned about spiritual gifts, had an opportunity to work at identifying their own spiritual gifts, and begun to identify just what their own place of service and ministry within the church might be.

Introduce yourself first, and then have the class members introduce themselves. You might have each class member say how long he or she has been
a member of your congregation and tell what has been his or her most re-
cent experience serving in a ministry either within your congregation, a
previous congregation, or in the community. Be prepared to hear both positive and negative experiences! One reason for this course is to enhance the
likelihood that persons will have positive ministry experiences as they serve
in the places that better utilize their God-given spiritual gifts.

Opening Prayer (2 minutes)

Offer this prayer or one like it:
Gracious God: We ask that you be with us during this adventure of explor-
ing our spiritual gifts. May we focus on ways that we might better serve you
and your people. Help us remember that our gifts have been given for your
glory and for the building of your Kingdom. In Christ's name we pray. Amen.

Introduce the Course (2 minutes)

Ask participants quickly to brainstorm reasons they have heard (or used
themselves) for why people do not volunteer to serve in the church. List
these on the white board or flipchart. Share that most of these reasons melt
away when a person's spiritual gifts are used and his or her passions are engaged in ministries.

The goal of this course is not the recruitment of volunteers. Instead, it is to
help people discover all the elements of who God created them to be and
to help them put those together to find an effective and fulfilling place of
service. S.T.R.I.D.E is an acronym used to capture those elements, which
we will explore together in this study. God has called all of us to serve, and
God has designed us in such a way that we each can serve in an area where
we will be not only capable but also happy to serve!

PLAY VIDEO: "Introduction and Biblical Foundation," segment 1 (5:23 minutes)

Study the Bible (25 minutes total)

Group Work (15 minutes)

Divide your group into an even number of smaller groups, each with three
to five members. Ask everyone to turn to pages 16-21in the workbook,

where the four foundational Bible passages dealing with spiritual gifts are found, each followed by a group of questions. Ask half of the groups to work on the questions dealing with 1 Corinthians 12 and Romans 12:1-8. Ask the other half of the groups to work on the questions dealing with Ephesians 4:1-16 and 1 Peter 4:9-11. If you have four or more groups, you may want to have each group work with a different passage. As they read the passages, have them underline in their books the names of the spiritual gifts listed. After making sure everyone understands the instructions, allow fifteen minutes for groups to work on these questions.

While the groups are working, prepare a chart like the one below on a white board or flipchart so that all participants can see it. (Note: Be sure to leave plenty of room for listing the spiritual gifts.)

Passage	Who receives the gifts?	For what purpose?	List of spiritual gifts
1 Corinthians 12			
Romans 12:1-8			
Ephesians 4:1-16			
1 Peter 4:9-11			

Review (10 minutes)

Stop the groups after fifteen minutes, even if they are not quite done. Then work through the questions together, allowing the group members to provide the answers as much as possible. As you go through the questions together, fill in the responses to the first two columns in the chart you have drawn on the white board or flipchart. (See the completed chart on page 18.) An answer key is provided here, based on the Today's New International Version of the Bible:

1 Corinthians 12

1. According to verse 1, what is Paul's desire regarding the subject of spiritual gifts? *That you not be uniformed. (Since this is written as a specific command here, understanding spiritual gifts must be important.)*

2. List and explain the contrasts found in verses 4-6. Hint: Look for the word *but. Who do you see at work here? Different kinds of gifts–same Spirit; different kinds of service–same Lord; different kinds of working–same God. Spirit-Lord-God implies the Trinity at work here. (It's important to note also that we see varieties–differences–but unity as well. This will come up again.*

3. According to verse 7, who receives the spiritual gifts, and for what purpose? *To each one is given . . . for the common good. (Who is "each"? The clues are in who wrote the letter and to whom it was written. It was written by Paul–a believer–to the church at Corinth–a group of believers.)*

4. What do verses 8-11 have to say about the giving of gifts? *They are given by the Spirit as the Spirit chooses. We don't choose which gift(s) we receive. (Also, we see again a variety of gifts being given; and no one individual receives all the gifts.)*

5. What analogy does Paul use with respect to gifts in verses 12-17? What does this analogy illustrate? Why do you think Paul chose to use it? *The human body. It uses the interdependence of the members of the body to illustrate that even though our spiritual gifts are different, we need each other for the whole church to function well. He probably used this because it was easy to understand.*

6. Who determines our place in the body of Christ according to verse 18? *God.*

7. What do we learn about the individual members of the body from verses 19-24? *All are important. All are indispensable.*

8. What is being said in verses 25-27 about our responsibility toward

one another? *There is no room for dissension or jealousy in the body. We are to care for one another.*

9. We learned in verses 8-11 that a variety of gifts are given. According to verses 28-30, is there any gift that is received by every member? *No. (The way these verses are worded in the Greek means the answer to this question is automatically "no.")*

Romans 12:1-8

1. What principles might Paul be trying to get across in verses 1-3? *There are several good teachings here: Serving God is an act of worship. (This one is key for our understanding spiritual gifts.) Do not be conformed to this world. Be transformed by the renewing of your minds. Think of yourself with sober judgment. God has assigned to each of us a measure of faith.*

2. According to verse 1, offering ourselves to God is true worship. How is using our spiritual gifts in service to God "true worship"? *It honors our unique God-design and fulfills God's purpose for our lives.*

3. What analogy does Paul reference again in verses 4-5? Why? What is his point? *Again, he uses the human body as an analogy for the church. He is saying that we do not have the same function, but we are one body in Christ. (There's that diversity with unity thing again!)*

4. According to verse 6, who receives the gifts? *Each of us.*

5. What do we learn about exercising our gifts from verses 6-8? *That our gifts differ according to the grace given us, and that we ought to exercise them accordingly—that is, according to the peculiar characteristics of that gift.*

Ephesians 4:1-16

1. What are the instructions given in verses 1-3? *Again, there are several: Lead a life worthy of your calling; be humble, gentle, patient, and forbearing with each other; maintain the unity of the Spirit. (Unity again–hmm, must be very important!)*

2. What are the seven characteristics common to all believers according to verses 4-6? What is the significance of this? *One body, one Spirit, one hope, one Lord, one faith, one baptism, one God. (Group members may come up with their own interpretations of this. We place a lot of importance sometimes on small differences among Christian practices. In the end, though, we have these seven essential characteristics of the Christian faith in common! We need to focus on the things that unite us, not the things that divide us.)*

3. Who receives the gifts according to verse 7? *Each one of us.*

4. For what purpose are gifts given according to verses 11-13? *To equip the saints for the work of ministry, for building up the body of Christ. (You might ask, "Who are the saints?" The answer is that we are. The word saints as used here refers to those who are sanctified through Christ.)*

5. What are the results in verses 14-16? *The church will grow together in love and not be misled by false teachings.*

1 Peter 4:9-11

1. What spiritual gift is listed in verse 9? *Hospitality.*

2. Who receives spiritual gifts, according to verse 10? *Each of you.*

3. How are spiritual gifts to be used? T*o serve one another and for the glory of God.*

4. What are the two categories of gifts found in this passage? *Speaking and serving.*

Identify the Spiritual Gifts (5 minutes)

Ask participants to go back into their same small groups. Have them turn to page 22 in their workbook. There they will find a chart where they are asked to "List the spiritual gifts you find in each of the Bible passages." Ask each group to complete the charts in their workbooks.

A completed chart based on Today's New International Version of the Bible would look like this:

1 Corinthians 12:8-10, 28-30	Romans 12:1-8	Ephesians 4:1-16	1 Peter 4:9-11
Message of Wisdom	Prophecy	Apostleship	Hospitality
Message of Knowledge	Serving (Helping)	Prophecy	
Faith	Teaching	Evangelism	
Gifts of Healing	Encouragement	Pastor-Teacher	
Miraculous Powers	Giving		
Prophecy	Leadership		
Distinguishing Between Spirits	Mercy		
Speaking in Different Kinds of Tongues			
Interpretation of Tongues			
Apostleship			
Teaching			
Helping (Serving			
Guidance (Administration)			

The purpose here is just to see what the Bible identifies as spiritual gifts. Some translations of the Bible may word them a little differently, but the essential meaning is the same. Note that in Ephesians 4:11, the way the text is written in Greek makes pastor-teacher one gift, as opposed to listing pastor as one gift and teacher as another.

Summarize Spiritual Gifts (5 minutes)

Now come back together as a full group, and work together to fill in the last column in the chart on the white board or flipchart. While you write responses on the chart, ask participants quickly to summarize what they have learned about spiritual gifts from Scripture.

Your completed chart will look like this:

Passage	Who receives the gifts?	For what purpose?	List of spiritual gifts
1 Corinthians 12	Each one	Common good	Message of Wisdom, Message of Knowledge, Faith, Gifts of Healing, Miraculous Powers, Prophecy, Distinguishing Between Spirits, Speaking in Tongues, Interpretation of Tongues, Apostles, Teachers, Helping (Serving), Guidance (Administration)
Romans 12:1-8	Each of us	True worship Part of the body	Prophecy, Mercy, Serving (Helping), Teaching, Encouragement, Giving, Leadership
Ephesians 4:1-16	Each one of us	Equip God's people for works of service, Build up the body of Christ	Apostles Prophets Evangelists Pastor-Teachers
1 Peter 4:9-11	Each of you	Serve others Glorify God	Hospitality Serving Speaking

**PLAY VIDEO, "Introduction and Biblical Foundation,"
second segment (4:01 minutes)**

Instructions for the Next Session (2 minutes)

- Read the material in Chapter 1 of the participant workbook.
- Complete the Spiritual Gifts Discovery Tool online or in the workbook before coming to class next week. The online Spiritual Gifts Discovery Tool (which will calculate all responses) can be found at: www.ministrymatters.com/spiritualgifts. Make certain that participants who choose to do the paper version of the discovery tool understand the instructions before they leave.

Closing Prayer (2 minutes)

Pray that God will watch over and guide the members of the group as they seek to discover and understand how God has gifted them in the coming weeks.

Session 2
Spiritual Gifts Defined

Objective for This Session:
To further understand the biblical foundation of spiritual gifts with the goal of gaining an appreciation for how they manifest themselves today.

Preparation: Read in advance Chapter 2 in the participant workbook and Session 2 in the leader guide. Read all Bible passages. Try all instructions given both in the workbook and in the leader guide.

Watch the DVD video segments "Spiritual Gifts Defined" and "Talents." (We recommend watching the segment on talents because questions about talents often come up during the discussion on spiritual gifts, and this segment will help you be prepared to respond.) If you are using overhead slides, either print the overheads for Session 2 for use on a projector or bring the disk to use with a computer and projector.

Materials Needed: blank nametags (if participants might still be unfamiliar with one another); pens or pencils; white board or flipchart with appropriate markers; participant workbooks

Welcome and Opening Prayer (2 minutes)

Welcome participants back and open with prayer, asking for God to send the Holy Spirit upon those gathered to help in understanding the gifts God gives in order to build up the church and to spread the good news of the love of God made known to us through Jesus Christ.

Debrief Spiritual Gifts Discovery Tool (3 minutes)

Ask participants to "pair and share" with someone next to them what their top three scores were on the Spiritual Gifts Discovery Tool. Give them one minute each for sharing. Encourage participants to focus on their highest scores regardless of what the scores are. Some people score themselves more conservatively than others. There is no threshold or minimum to be reached. Were they surprised, or did it seem a perfect fit to them?

PLAY VIDEO: "Spiritual Gifts Defined," first segment (5 minutes)

Work Through the Definitions and Uses of Spiritual Gifts (35 minutes total)

Group Work (20 minutes)

Ask participants to form small groups with three to five members in each group. Draw their attention to pages 33-58 in the workbook, where they will find definitions of the twenty spiritual gifts mentioned in the Bible. (The definitions also may be found on pages 43-61 in this book.) Give them about twenty minutes for this assignment. As groups, their tasks are:

• To read through the definition of each spiritual gift. (They do not have to read through each biblical reference unless they feel it would help their understanding; they will not have time to read all of the Bible passages listed during the time allotted for this learning activity. Stagger where the small groups begin reading in the list to ensure that all the spiritual gifts will be covered by at least one, if not all, groups.)

• To come to an understanding of what each spiritual gift might look like and how it might be used within the church today.

• To discuss whether anyone in the group knows of anyone else inside or outside of the congregation whom they think might have that particular spiritual gift and how they might be encouraged in their exercise of it.

Each small group should work their way as far through the spiritual gifts as time allows. Make sure they are aware of the time constraints and encourage them not to spend too much time discussing any one gift.

Summarize (15 minutes)

After bringing the small groups back together, ask each group to report on what each spiritual gift might look like in the church today, or to choose someting interesting they learned about each of the gists they studied and highlight themfor the whole group.

PLAY VIDEO: "Spiritual Gifts Defined," second segment (2:45 minutes)

Instructions for the Next Session (2 minutes)

Read Chapter 3 and answer all questions contained within the chapter.

Closing Prayer (2 minutes)

Pray that God will bring insight into God's plan for the participants' lives as they continue to explore and develop their spiritual gifts.

Session 3
Talents and Resources

Objective for This Session:
To gain an understanding of talents as distinguished from spiritual gifts and to see how your resources can affect your ministry within the church.

Preparation: Read in advance Chapter 3 in the participant workbook and Session 3 in the leader guide. Try all instructions given both in the workbook and in the leader guide.

Watch again the DVD video segment "Talents" and also the video segment "Resources." If you are using overhead slides, either print the overheads for Session 3 for use on a projector or bring the disk for use with a computer and projector.

Materials Needed: blank paper; pens or pencils; white board or flipchart with appropriate markers; participant workbooks

Welcome and Opening Prayer (2 minutes)

Welcome participants back and open with prayer, asking for God to nurture the gifts and talents given to the unique individuals gathered in this place that they might serve to build up the body of Christ and lead more people to Christ's love.

PLAY VIDEO: "Talents" (4:35 minutes)

Distinguish Talents from Spiritual Gifts (10 minutes)

Review the list of persons on page 61 in the workbook and what their talents are. Possible answers might include:

Peyton Manning –football, sports;
Celine Dion – singing, performing;
Bill Gates – computers, technology, entrepreneurship, charity;
John Grisham – writing, law

Discuss the differences between talents and spiritual gifts. Talents and gifts can be very similar and even overlap, but there are some key differences:

Spiritual Gifts	Talents
Received by every Christian	Received by every human
Beyond natural ability	Natural ability (or acquired skill)
Always used to serve others and to glorify God	May be used to serve others and to glorify God, but can also be used for own purposes

Your class may come up with others. Acquired abilities are those skills we gain through training or experience. Some examples are public speaking, facilitation skills, accounting skills, and computer skills. Remind the group not to get caught up in the distinction between gifts and talents; God can use BOTH to accomplish God's purposes in the world.

Begin to Identify Talents (10 minutes)

Ask participants to brainstorm what talents or acquired skills they think they might have that could be used in service to Christ. Write those down on the white board or flipchart. Talk as a group in a general discussion about how they might be nurtured and offered in service through the church.

It's time to switch gears and explore the topic of resources.

PLAY VIDEO: "Resources" (3:35 minutes)

Explore the Concept of Resources (10 minutes)

It's natural for us to think of financial resources when we talk about using our resources to serve others through the body of Christ. Our resources, though, do include our time, our material possessions, our contacts, and our hobbies. Ask participants to brainstorm what they have in their own lives that might be considered resources. Write these resources on the white board or flipchart as they call them out. These first responses may spark ideas for other participants.

Time is a critical component of the resources we have to offer. Ask the group to list reasons it is so important to objectively evaluate the time we have to offer as we consider a potential ministry role. Write these reasons on the white board or flipchart as they call them out.

Work on a Personal Summary Picture (10 minutes)

Distribute sheets of paper to each participant. In order to help summarize what persons have learned about themselves thus far (halfway through the course) and also to help those persons who learn best through images rather than words, tell participants that they will be drawing a summary picture of themselves to represent their spiritual gifts, talents, and resources. Realizing that not everyone has the talent of drawing, the picture need not be elaborate and can be as simple as a stick figure and very rough, symbolic approximations of things. The person might be depicted using a talent, having a spiritual gift "inside," and being surrounded by resources. So, for example, we might have a simple drawing of a person sitting at a piano (talent of piano playing), with an exclamation point drawn inside the person's head area (spiritual gift of wisdom), and with a cabin to one side of the person (resource of a cabin that could be used by church groups for retreats).

Depending on available time, participants can include as many of their talents, spiritual gifts, and resources in their drawings as they are able.

Be sure to allow time for persons to share what they have drawn.

Instructions for the Next Session (2 minutes)

Read Chapter 4 and answer all questions contained within the chapter.

Closing Prayer (2 minutes)

Pray that the participants might gain deeper insight in the next week as they reflect on their talents and resources and how those might be used to further God's kingdom.

Session 4
Individuality

Objective for This Session:
To discover one's own individuality and the implications for the ways personal style can affect serving God in church and community.

Preparation: Read in advance Chapter 4 in the participant workbook and Session 4 in the leader guide. Read all Bible passages. Try all instructions given both in the workbook and in the leader guide.

Watch the DVD video segment "Individuality." If you are using the overhead slides, either print the overheads for Session 4 for use on a projector or bring the disk for use with a computer and projector.

Materials Needed: pens or pencils; white board or flipchart with appropriate markers; participant workbooks

Welcome and Opening Prayer (2 minutes)

Welcome participants back and open with prayer, asking for God to bless the unique ways we serve others and glorify God.

PLAY VIDEO: "Individuality," first segment (6:31 minutes)

Understanding the Concept (30 minutes total)

Note: While our individual personalities and preferences help to make each one of us unique, no type is better or worse than any other. However, personality traits might make individuals better suited for particular ways of serving and less so for others. It is because of this that understanding our own individuality becomes so important and helpful. We will be more joyful and effective if we serve in ways that mesh better with our own unique personality, even though we might stretch ourselves to serve in ways that do not exactly match if the need arises.

Identifying Your Energy Focus (15 minutes)

On the white board or flipchart, draw a horizontal line. Label the line "Energy Focus." Mark "Extrovert" at the left end and "Introvert" at the right end. Explain that one of the two important components of Individuality that we will look at today is a very broad description of personality type. A number of psychologists including Carl Jung, Isabel Briggs-Myers, and David Keirsey have written about the differences between introverts and extroverts and their energy sources. Members of the class may have taken the Myers-Briggs Type Indicator or the Keirsey Temperament Sorter. Ask members who have taken such assessments what they learned about themselves.

Ask: What are the differences between introverts and extroverts? Remind participants that it's not so much shyness vs. being outgoing; it's a matter of how one receives and expends energy. Are we drained of energy by being among people so that we have to go off by ourselves for a while to recover? Or are we energized by people but then go bonkers if we are stuck by ourselves for too long? That's the primary distinction between introverts and extroverts.

Ask participants to review or work individually on the questions on pages 71-72 in the workbook, which deal with energy focus. Allow about five minutes.

Check to see if anyone is still unsure whether he or she is an extrovert or an introvert. If anyone is unsure, ask that person's permission to allow the group to help in figuring out that person's energy focus from his or her responses to the questions.

Ask participants to mark where they would place themselves on the Extrovert-Introvert continuum on page 72 of the workbook.

Understanding Your Preferred Environment (15 minutes)

On the white board or flipchart, draw a vertical line intersecting the "Energy Focus" horizontal line you have already drawn. Label the line, "Preferred Environment." Mark "Flexible" at the top, and "Stable" at the bottom.

Explain that the other important component of Individuality involves our preferred environment. Specifically, how do we feel about structure in our work? Do we want everything to be laid out and predictable? Or do we want to be independent as we do things? This is the realm of stability vs. flexibility.

Ask participants to review or work individually on the questions on pages 73-75 in the workbook, which deal with preferred environment. Allow about five minutes.

Check to see if anyone is still unsure whether he or she prefers stability or flexibility. If anyone is unsure, ask that person's permission to allow the group to help in figuring out that person's preferred environment from his or her responses to the questions.

Ask participants to mark where they would place themselves on the Flexible-Stable continuum on page 75 of the workbook.

Putting the Components Together (15 minutes total)

Visualizing the Varieties (3 minutes)

You have already drawn two axes on the white board or flipchart. Ask participants to come up to the chart and write their initials roughly where their location would be on each axis. This will help them to see that there are varying degrees within each component. Combining the choices from the Energy Focus axis and the Preferred Environment axis, you have four possible combinations: extroverts who prefer stability, extroverts who prefer flexibility, introverts who prefer stability, and introverts who prefer flexibility. Because of differing degrees in each area, even persons who share the same combination will still be unique individuals. The closer one is toward the center of each axis, the more likely one may be able to take on the characteristics of another type as the need arises.

PLAY VIDEO: "Individuality," second segment (1:07 minutes)

Type Discussion (5 minutes)

Ask persons who share an energy focus/preferred environment combination to form small groups together. If a particular one of the four groups has too many participants in it, you might want to split that group into even smaller groups. One-member groups are okay for this activity. The assignment is to read over and discuss as a group the material found on pages 76-78 in the workbook pertaining to their particular combination. Small groups should discuss (1) whether the description fits their experience, (2) whether they feel drawn to the church ministries suggested for that combination, and (3) what they think of the word of caution given for that combination.

Debrief and Summarize (5 minutes)

Ask the groups to take one minute each and summarize their discussion.

Instructions for the Next Session (2 minutes)

Read Chapter 5 and answer all questions contained within the chapter.

Closing Prayer (2 minutes)

Pray that God will bless the participants as they embrace and rejoice in how God has made each of them unique individuals.

For more reading about personality types described around energy, organizing, and information needs, see:

Please Understand Me II: Temperament, Character, Intelligence, Peter Keirsey, Prometheus Nemesis Book Company, May 1998.

Gifts Differing, Isabel Briggs-Myers, Consulting Psychologists Press, August 1980.

Groups and individuals can arrange to take the Myers-Briggs Type Indicator through a certified trainer in your area. Briefer, less statistical testing tools often can be found on the Internet.

Session 5
Dreams

Objective for This Session:
To begin the work of discovering the particular dream or passion God has placed in each person's heart.

Preparation: Read in advance Chapter 5 in the participant workbook and Session 5 in the leader guide. Try all instructions given both in the workbook and in the leader guide.

You will need to prepare according to one of two plans for the activity "Be Touched by a Dream." In Plan A, you will be projecting the color slides for the group. This will require you to use the DVD with a laptop computer, LCD projector, and screen to show the slide show. Or you may print the slide show on overhead transparency slides and project them with an overhead projector. Plan B will require you to use the DVD to print out a set of the pictures from the slide show. You will then need, in advance, to post those pictures at eye level around the room or, preferably, in a nearby area. NOTE: The DVD will allow you to insert pictures of ministries and activities from your own church or community. We encourage you to do this, as seeing something familiar, and perhaps locally relevant, will sometimes help people connect better with what they see.

Watch the DVD video segment "Dreams." If you are using the overhead slides, either print the overheads for Session 5 for use on a projector or bring the disk for use with a computer and projector.

Materials Needed: blank paper; pens or pencils, white board or flipchart with appropriate markers; participant workbooks; for Plan A: the DVD, a laptop computer, an LCD projector, and a projection screen or transparencies and an overhead projector; for Plan B: a set of pictures from the DVD, printed out and posted in advance.

Welcome and Opening Prayer (2 minutes)

Welcome participants back and open with prayer, thanking God for spiritual gifts, talents, resources, individual styles, and dreams that assist us in finding the best ways to serve God.

PLAY VIDEO: "Dreams" (6:15 minutes)

Be Touched by a Dream (45 minutes total)

Plan A

Slide Show (10 minutes)

Ask participants to turn to the "Be Touched by a Dream" form on page 89 in Chapter 5 of the workbook. Tell the participants that you will be showing them thirty-three pictures. As they watch the pictures, they are to keep track of which ones "grab" them or engage them. They are not to think about the pictures or analyze them; rather, they are to pay attention to how they feel about them. Participants should put a check or "x" beside the number of each picture that engages them. They also might write a few words about what touched them. Show the pictures without comment, changing pictures every fifteen seconds.

Descriptions (20 minutes)

After showing the slides or viewing the pictures, read aloud the descriptions of each of the thirty-three pictures (see page 34). Ask participants to jot down descriptions beside the pictures that particularly moved them. Afterward, give participants time to look over their lists individually. Ask them to look over the words they jotted down. Do they see any patterns in the photos they chose? If patterns do show up, those patterns might indicate a dream or a passion. For example, if the word hunger shows up several times on someone's sheet of paper because he or she was moved by several pictures of people suffering from hunger, perhaps that individual has been given a dream—a passion—of working in some way to combat hunger. Or maybe another individual notes that she or he has mentioned several different kinds of carpentry tools that showed up in pictures. That might mean that this person has a passion that could be fulfilled by working with a volunteer mission team on a construction project or with a Habitat for Humanity housing project. If participants can't readily identify a dream they have, suggest they start with eliminating some things they do NOT feel passionately about. For instance, perhaps they don't want to work with young children, or they're not particularly passionate about women's issues. Remind them that this is okay; sometimes it takes trial and error (and some exposure to different opportunities) to find the one thing that gets them engaged.

Group Time (15 minutes)

Next, divide the participants into groups of three persons. Each person will have five minutes to share his or her insights into what his or her dreams and passions might be. If time allows within the five minutes, she or he may invite feedback from the other two members of the small group; however, the full five minutes is to be focused on that individual's dreams and passions. You as leader will need to keep strict track of time in order to tell participants when it is time to move to the second and the third group members.

Plan B

Plan B is the same as Plan A, except that instead of viewing the DVD slide show, participants will view posted pictures with the same set of instructions. Allow ten minutes for viewing the pictures.

Proceed with the same directions as for Plan A.

Instructions for the Next Session (2 minutes)

Read Chapter 6 in the participant workbook. Ask group members to consider how the insights they gain from working through Chapter 6 mesh with the insights they have gained from this session.

Closing Prayer (2 minutes)

Ask God to provide clarity to the dreams and callings of these people.

Be Touched by a Dream: Descriptions

Show the slides or printouts to participants with little information or explanation so that they can record their emotional response to the pictures. After the participants have seen the slides or printouts and checked the pictures that engaged them, read aloud the following descriptions. First, a description reminds the viewers of the images in the photo, and then the words in italics suggest the possibilities of what may have appealed, including the type of individual helped (a child), a particular issue (health care), or a role of service (administrator, teacher). The descriptions do not cover all the concepts in each picture, and some pictures can be interpreted several ways; so expect some discussions.

1. Group of women with Bibles	*Women's Bible study, Women's ministry*
2. Child painting	*Children's ministry, Arts-based ministry*
3. Older and younger man walking	*Senior adult ministry*
4. People carrying building materials	*Building ministry, Missions*
5. Group of men with Bibles	*Men's ministry, Bible study*
6. View of choir from congregation	*Choir, Music ministry, Worship*
7. Men in hard hats working	*Maintenance*
8. Man putting money in offering plate	*Giving, Financial ministry*
9. Woman working at a desk	*Administration*
10. Serving food in a kitchen	*Food ministry*
11. Praying around an open Bible	*Bible study, Prayer*
12. Folding bulletins	*Administration, Bulletin preparation*
13. Man directing traffic	*Traffic, Parking*
14. Visiting in the hospital	*Hospital ministry, Hospice*
15. Cell phone and computer	*Media, Technology*
16. Pouring coffee	*Coffee, Hospitality*
17. Woman interacting with young children	*Children's ministry*
18. Woman tutoring girl	*Tutoring, Children and youth*
19. Playing music in a nursing home	*Music ministry, Nursing home*
20. Two women with food in a kitchen	*Hospitality, Food ministry*
21. Minister praying over sick person	*Hospital ministry, Hospice*
22. Doctor treating baby in mission field	*Medical missions*
23. Musicians playing on street	*Music ministry*
24. Man teaching/preaching in sanctuary	*Teaching, Preaching*
25. Woman holding books	*Library, Bookstore*
26. Men praying	*Men's group, Prayer ministry*
27. Man preaching/teaching to large group	*Preaching, Teaching*
28. Group working construction	*Building ministry, Habitat*
29. Girl in wheelchair talking with friend	*Youth, Special needs*
30. Greeting people in worship	*Greeting, Welcome*
31. Men and women reading Bibles together	*Bible study, Teaching, Home groups*
32. Group of senior adults	*Senior adult ministry*
33. Group of yong adults by the water	*Young adult, College ministry*

__Note to Leader:__ Note that viewers may agree or disagree with the position expressed in the slide, but they are to ask themselves: Does it inspire the desire to speak out as a person of faith—either for or against important issues?

Session 6
Experiences

Objective for This Session:
To consider how God can use our past experiences for God's purposes.

Preparation: Read in advance Chapter 6 in the participant workbook and Session 6 in the leader guide. Try all instructions given both in the workbook and in the leader guide.

Make sure there is plenty of table work space for the "Tapestry of My Life" activity.

Watch the DVD video segment "Experiences." If you are using overhead slides, either print the overheads for Session 6 for use on a projector or bring the disk for use with a computer and projector.

Materials Needed: blank paper; pens or pencils; colorful construction paper; small blank stickers for each participant, approximately 1" x ¾" (available at any office supply store or stores that sell school supplies); participant workbooks

Welcome and Opening Prayer (3 minutes)

Welcome participants back and open with prayer, praising God as the God of the past as well as of the present and the future.

Review Dreams and Passions (5 minutes)

Ask participants to share briefly about further insights they have had since the last meeting about their dreams and passions, especially as they read and worked through the material in Chapter 6 in the workbook.

PLAY VIDEO: "Experiences" (5:11 minutes)

Learn from Experiences (40 minutes total)

Tapestry of My Life: Worksheet (10 minutes)

Divide the class into groups of three or four people each. Ask participants to turn to the "Tapestry of My Life" exercise on pages 93-94 in their workbooks. (A copy of the page is also included on the DVD so that you can print out extra copies to have on hand.) The exercise worksheet has a space for the participant to write his or her name, and five blank "bubbles." Ask participants to think of at least five significant accomplishments or important events in their lives so far. At least one of these should be a negative or disappointing experience that they came through, survived, or conquered. Instruct them to write a few key words or phrases about each of those experiences in one of the bubbles.

Allow no more than ten minutes for the completion of the charts. You'll need the rest of the time to complete the exercise!

Tapestry of My Life: Group Sharing Time (25 minutes)

When the charts are finished, distribute blank sheets of paper or construction paper and stickers. Each participant in the group will write his or her name on a page. Then, in turn, each group member will read his or her five experiences to the group. While they listen, using their stickers, the other group members will write on the stickers suggestions about strengths and traits the person speaking exhibited during this particular experience. Then the group will pass around the reader's page and put their stickers on the page. As they place the stickers on the page, group members are to verbally affirm the person with positive comments relating to the person's experiences.

For example, a person may share that he graduated from college with honors. The experience may be described as significant because the student worked his way through school as well as gained scholarships and paid for the entire education. It had taught him the value of education and of hard work, but also had given him confidence in himself. Other participants, after hearing about this experience, might jot down the following traits or strengths on stickers and attach them to his timeline while making affirming comments such as these:

Perseverance—"You stuck with it!"

Intelligence—"You were able to work a job and display academic excellence."
Independence—"It's great that you did this on your own."

Tapestry of My Life: Debriefing (5 minutes)

Wrap up with a debriefing time: What did group members learn through the exercise? How did it make them feel? You'll likely hear things like:
- "God DID bring something good out of my bad experiences!"
- "I feel affirmed and good about myself."
- "Others see strengths in me that I wasn't even aware of!"

Instructions for the Next (Recommended but Optional) Session (2 minutes)

- No assignment, but ask participants to bring their workbooks with them, as you'll be putting together everything they've learned to better understand the importance of finding their unique S.T.R.I.D.E. as they seek to know, love, and serve God better.

Closing Prayer (2 minutes)

Offer thanks and praise to God, for being a God who knows everything about us—the good, the bad, and the ugly—and loves us still. Pray that God will use all that the participants have learned in this class to bring home the truth that we are all gifted, loved children of God, and that ALL have something important to offer to the body of Christ. Ask for God's blessings and guidance as participants seek to know, love, and serve God better.

Putting It All Together
and Making a Connection

Objective for This Session:
To think about how all the S.T.R.I.D.E. components can help us understand where God wants us to be in ministry and, for those who feel ready, to take the next step toward one-on-one ministry placement consultations.

Preparation: Prepare by reading in advance Chapter 7 in the participant workbook and Session 7 in the leader guide. Fill out the S.T.R.I.D.E. Ministry Profile form yourself. Print out and make enough copies of the Ministry Matching Exercise from the DVD for each participant.

Watch the DVD video segment "Putting It All Together." If you are using overhead slides, either print the overheads for Session 7 for use on a projector or bring the disk for use with a computer and projector.

Make sure that you or someone else from your church is prepared to follow up by offering one-on-one ministry placement consultations with those participants who wish them. It is vitally important that persons who have identified their spiritual gifts, talents, resources, individuality, dreams, and experiences be quickly matched up with an area in which they can serve other people to the glory of God.

Materials Needed: pens or pencils; white board or flipchart with appropriate markers; laptop and projector or overhead projector (if using slides); participant workbooks

Welcome and Opening Prayer (2 minutes)

Welcome participants back and open with prayer, thanking God for the opportunity to serve God through helping other people.

PLAY VIDEO: "Putting It All Together" (2:58 minutes)

Complete the S.T.R.I.D.E. Ministry Profile (5 minutes)

Tell participants to turn to the S.T.R.I.D.E. Ministry Profile on pages 99-100 of the workbook. Based on all they have learned about themselves through *Serving from the Heart*, ask participants to fill out their Ministry Profile.

You may want to note on the white board or flipchart that they can locate information they wrote about themselves in previous sessions on these pages in their workbooks:

Spiritual Gifts: pages 29, 58
Talents: page 63
Resources: page 66
Individuality: pages 71-72, 74-75
Dreams: pages 84-86
Experiences: page 93

Tell them to skip over the section for "Three Possible Areas of Ministry Involvement" at this time. However, if they are already serving in a ministry position, they should complete the line that begins, "I am already involved in the ministry area of. . . ."

For the moment, they should hold on to their completed S.T.R.I.D.E. Ministry Profile form.

See How Matching People with Ministries Works (25 minutes)

Divide participants into small groups of three to five persons. Distribute copies of the Ministry Matching Exercise to each participant. Each small group is now to take on the role of the Ministry Matching Team of a congregation. Their task is to discuss and come to some consensus about what kinds of spiritual gifts, talents, resources, individuality, dreams, and experiences they might look for in a person they would want to match up with each of the ministries on the sheet. Ask each group to begin with a different ministry position identified on the handout.

If a group has time, persons within the group may discuss to what extent they are suited to serve in one of the ministry positions described on the sheet according to the S.T.R.I.D.E. components or guidelines they have just written.

Debrief (10 minutes)

Bring the full group back together and ask what insights they received from the Ministry Matching Exercise. Did they see how one component of a person's S.T.R.I.D.E. could make a difference in whether the position was a good "fit"? What other thoughts did they have?

Wrap Up (5 minutes)

Be sure that persons have marked on their Ministry Profile forms whether they want a one-on-one ministry placement consultation. Explain that if they mark "yes," either you or someone else from the congregation will contact them to spend time going over their profile in detail and suggesting specific ways in which they might be of service within their church or community. Ask participants to give you their S.T.R.I.D.E. Ministry Profile forms.

Closing Prayer (2 minutes)

Pray that whatever comes from the service and ministry of the people in this course, it will be for God's glory alone.

A Special Note on the Placement Process

At Church of the Resurrection, we have teams of people who serve in our Connections Ministry. They are passionate about helping people find many types of connections in our congregation—in study, in community life, or in service. They are well informed about the various opportunities in our church and our community. One of the Connections Ministry teams, the Spiritual Gifts Placement Team, works specifically on follow-up regarding the gifts of class graduates.

Our ministry leaders have developed ministry position descriptions for each of the ministries at Church of the Resurrection, and the Spiritual Gifts Placement Team uses these while working with Serving from the Heart graduates to help them make a connection. This is accomplished in one of many ways, but the two ways it happens most frequently are as follows:

1) After the close of the last session, the S.T.R.I.D.E. ministry profiles are given to the Spiritual Gifts Placement Team, and members of

that team follow up with those participants who indicated they wanted to make a connection. They call or e-mail to set up one-on-one meetings.

2) Occasionally during the last session we will reduce the amount of time spent on the Ministry Matching exercise to one ministry position per group. This allows us to invite several members of the Spiritual Gifts Placement Team to come into the classroom and meet in a corner of the room with a small group of participants. They will spend thirty to sixty minutes with their groups, brainstorming potential matches based on their S.T.R.I.D.E. ministry profiles.

Members of the Spiritual Gifts Placement Team also facilitate the connection of the class graduates to the appropriate ministry leaders for follow-up. The ministry leaders receive e-mail or paper forms with the names and contact information of the graduates, the information from their S.T.R.I.D.E. profiles, and the service roles in which the graduates are interested. The ministry leaders are asked to contact the graduates interested in their areas within seventy-two hours.

Your ministry placement process may look different, but it is incredibly important! People are much more likely to follow through with serving if they have some help facilitating a connection—and if they have a contact who will help them find a new position if they should find that their first ministry position isn't the right fit.

Several examples of the forms and documents used in our placement process are included on the DVD. These may help you if you do not already have a placement process at your church.

May God bless you and your ministry as you help people find their S.T.R.I.D.E. serving God!

Spiritual Gifts—Definitions

Administration (Guidance)

*Greek: kybernēsis = pilotage, to steer, a guide,
directorship in the church*

The spiritual gift of Administration (or Guidance) is the God-given ability to organize and manage information, people, events, and resources to accomplish the objectives of a ministry. People with this gift handle details carefully and thoroughly. They are skilled in determining priorities, and in planning and directing the steps needed to achieve a goal. They feel frustrated when faced with disorder, and are uncomfortable with inefficiency. People with the gift of Administration often make it easier for others to use their own gifts, simply by keeping things organized and flowing smoothly.

Administration is about efficiency.

Adjectives that may describe a person with the gift of Administration are:

Conscientious	Efficient	Dependable
Objective	Organized	Thorough
	Goal-oriented	

Apostleship

Greek: apostolos = a delegate, a special ambassador of the gospel,
officially a commissioner of Christ,
a messenger, one who is sent

The divine ability to build the foundation of new churches by preaching the word, teaching others to live by Christ's commandments through the example of their own lives, and preparing the people to serve one another. Persons with the gift of Apostleship are not only eager to bring the gospel to those who have never heard it; they prepare those people to continue the work after they have left. They enthusiastically approach new ministries, churches, or settings, and realize the need to adapt methods of evangelism and service to widely different environments. People with this gift might envision themselves as missionaries, but some may not—they may instead accept and exercise leadership over a number of new churches or ministries.

Apostleship is about new ministries.

Adjectives that may describe a person with the gift of Apostleship are:

Entrepreneurial	Cause-driven	Risk-taking
Adaptable	Persevering	Adventurous
	Culturally sensitive	

Distinguishing of Spirits

Greek: diakrisis = judicial estimation, discerning
pneuma = a current of air, figuratively "a spirit," mental disposition

    The divine ability to recognize what is of God and what is not of God—to distinguish between good and evil, truth and error, and pure motives and impure motives. People with this gift usually can rely on instincts or first impressions to tell when a person or message is deceptive or inconsistent with biblical truths. They can sense the presence of evil, and they question motives, intentions, doctrine, deeds, and beliefs. These people must take care to use their gift in a way that brings good to the body of Christ—to judge with mercy and understanding rather than to condemn. It is unfortunate that people sometimes use this gift as a weapon against someone they disagree with, as opposed to seeking to understand whether their feeling is truly Spirit led.

Distinguishing of Spirits is about clarity.

Adjectives that may describe a person with the gift of Distinguishing of Spirits are:

Insightful	Truthful	Confronting
Intuitive	Receptive	Perceptive
	Decisive	

Encouragement

Greek: paraklēsis = imploration, solace, comfort, exhortation, entreaty

The God-given ability to encourage, help, intercede for, and be an advocate for others in a way that motivates others to grow in their faith and urges them to action. Encouragement (also referred to as Exhortation) takes many forms, and can be done through personal relationships, music, writings, intercessory prayer, and speaking, to name a few. People with this gift encourage others to remain faithful, even in the midst of struggles. They are sensitive and sympathetic toward another person's emotional state and exhort selflessly, with affection, not contempt. They can see positive traits or aspects that other persons overlook and often have more faith in other persons than they have in themselves.

Encouragement is about exhortation.

Adjectives that may describe a person with the gift of Encouragement are:

Affirming	Motivating	Consoling
Challenging	Reassuring	Comforting
	Positive	

Evangelism

Greek: euagelistēs = a preacher of the gospel

The divine ability to spread the good news of Jesus Christ so that unknowing persons respond with faith and discipleship. Contrary to what you might think, people with the gift of Evangelism do not all speak of their faith from a podium or by taking their message door-to-door through a neighborhood, though some do. Most people with this gift simply speak comfortably about their faith; nonbelievers are drawn into this circle of comfort. These people enjoy many friendships outside of their Christian community. They enjoy helping others see how Christianity can fulfill their needs. They eagerly study questions that challenge Christianity. They respond clearly in ways that connect with individuals—meeting the individuals right where they are.

Evangelism is about the good news.

Adjectives that may describe a person with the gift of Evangelism are:

Confident	Relational	Faith-sharing
Outgoing	Spiritual Communicator	Challenging

Faith

***Greek: pistis = faith in God, a personal surrender to God
with a conduct inspired by such surrender,
moral conviction, assurance***

The divine ability to recognize what God wants done, and to act when others fall back in doubt. Although as Christians we are all called to have faith, people with the spiritual gift of Faith receive it in an extraordinary measure. Even in the face of barriers that overwhelm others, people with this gift simply have confidence that God will see God's will done. Believing deeply in the power of prayer, they also know that God is both present and active in their lives. People with this gift, by their works and by their words, show others that God is faithful to God's promises.

Faith is about confidence.

Adjectives that may describe a person with the gift of Faith are:

Prayerful   Assured   Trusting
Illuminating   Optimistic   Convinced
                     Hopeful

Giving

Greek: metadidōmi = to give over, share, impart

The God-given ability to give material wealth freely and joyfully, knowing that spiritual wealth will abound as God's work is advanced. Those with the gift of Giving are not always affluent but are always generous with what they DO have. People with this gift usually manage their finances well, may have a special ability to make money, and tend to be frugal in their lifestyle. They use these skills to increase their support for God's work, and trust that God will provide for their needs. They are often comfortable and successful in approaching others for gifts. Instead of asking, "How much of my money do I give to God?" they ask, "How much of God's money do I keep?"

Giving is about resources.

Adjectives that may describe a person with the gift of Giving are:

Charitable	Generous	Responsible
Disciplined	Depends on God	Good steward
	Resourceful	

Healing

Greek: charisma = a spiritual endowment, a divine gratuity, a religious qualification
iama = cures, healings

The divine ability to bring wholeness—physical, emotional, or spiritual—to others. People with this gift listen skillfully as they seek God's guidance to learn the needs of the sick and to determine the causes and nature of an illness. They believe that God can cure and that prayer can overcome any negative forces at work (but they also recognize that God might have a different plan). Their tools include prayer, touch, and spoken words. This gift shows God's power; at the same time, it is to God's glory. The goal of healing is not just healing itself, but spreading the gospel by pointing to the power of Jesus Christ and to show the glory of God.

Healing is about wholeness.

Adjectives that may describe a person with the gift of Healing are:

Faith-filled	Powerful in prayer	Submissive
Compassionate	Spiritual	Humble
	Trusts in God	

Helps (Serving)

Greek: diakonia = attendance, aid, relief, service, ministry

The God-given ability to work alongside others in performing practical and often behind-the-scenes tasks to sustain and enhance the body of Christ. A person with this gift receives spiritual satisfaction from doing everyday necessary tasks; he or she may prefer to work quietly and without public recognition. When a need is seen, the helper frequently takes care of it without being asked. The helper's work often frees up other persons so that they may carry out their own ministries.

Helps is about assistance.

Adjectives that may describe a person with the gift of Helps are:

Available	Reliable	Pragmatic
Dependable	Willing	Selfless
	Servant-oriented	

Hospitality

Greek: philoxenos = fond of guests, i.e. hospitable, given to hospitality

The divine ability to make others feel welcome and comfortable. People with the gift of hospitality often love to entertain. Sometimes, however, their gift is simply demonstrated by a warm handshake or hug, a bright smile, and a tendency to greet new people and help them get acclimated to a new place or situation. People are drawn to persons with this gift—they often have many acquaintances or friends and help others make connections, too.

Hospitality is about welcoming.

Adjectives that may describe a person with the gift of Hospitality are:

Warm   Generous   Inviting
Open   Social

Message of Knowledge

Greek: logos = something said, utterance, communication
gnōsis = knowledge

The God-given ability to understand, organize, and effectively use or communicate information to advance God's purposes. The information may come either from the Holy Spirit or from sources around us. People with this gift enjoy studying the Bible and other sources to gain facts, insights, and truths. The term "message of knowledge" is intentional. This gift is not knowledge for one's own benefit—it must be communicated and shared with others. People with this gift use their knowledge for projects, ministries, or teaching. They organize it in order to pass it to other persons for their use and benefit. The Holy Spirit appears to be at work when these people show unusual insight or understanding.

Message of Knowledge is about awareness.

Adjectives that may describe a person with the gift of Message of Knowledge are:

Comprehending	Astute	Rational
Observant	Diligent	Reflective
	Studious	

Leadership

Greek: proistēmi = to stand before,
to preside, maintain, be over

The divine ability to motivate, coordinate, and direct people doing God's work. People with this gift are visionaries who inspire others to work together to make the vision a reality. They take responsibility for setting and achieving goals; they step in where there is a lack of direction. They build a team of talented persons, and then they empower them. These persons are called to be servant-leaders. Held to a high moral standard, they lead by the example of their own lives.

Leadership is about direction.

Adjectives that may describe a person with the gift of Leadership are:

Diligent	Visionary	Persuasive
Influential	Role model	Activating
	Inspiring	

Mercy

Greek: eleeō = to have compassion, to have mercy on

The God-given ability to see and feel the suffering of others and to minister to them with love and understanding. More simply, this gift is "compassion in action." People with this gift are called to reach out to someone who is hurt or rejected, easing his or her suffering. They feel fulfilled when they can show others that God loves them. They are skilled at gaining the trust of those in need and enjoy finding ways to comfort them.

Mercy is about care.

Adjectives that may describe a person with the gift of Mercy are:

Empathetic	Tender	Sensitive
Responsive	Kind	Caring
	Burden-bearing	

Pastor — Teacher

Greek: poimēn = a shepherd
didaskalos = an instructor, master, teacher

The divine ability to guide, protect, and care for other people as they experience spiritual growth. People with this gift enjoy working with groups of people and nurturing their growth over an extended period of time. Because of these long-term relationships, they establish trust and confidence and are able to take the time to care for the "whole person." They can assess where a person is spiritually and then develop or find places where that person can continue his or her journey of faith. They model compassion. The phrase for this gift in the original Greek indicates one gift— "pastor-teacher," not two gifts, "pastor" and "teacher." The primary difference between a pastor-teacher (or shepherd) and a teacher seems to be the longer-term, holistic care provided (in addition to instruction) by a shepherd, versus a teacher, who may operate in a shorter-term aspect, imparting knowledge and instruction, but not necessarily care.

Pastor-Teacher is about shepherding.

Adjectives that may describe a person with the gift of Pastor-Teacher are:

Nuturing	Disciple-maker	Guiding
Relational	Protective	Facilitating
	Instructing	

Distinguishing of Spirits

Greek: prophēteuō = speak under inspiration,
speak forth the mind and counsel of God

The God-given ability, out of love for God's people, to proclaim God's truth in a way that makes it relevant to current situations in today's culture and guides others to more faith-informed decisions and actions. The goal is not to condemn, but to bring about change or enlightenment. People with this gift listen carefully to God so their words will be God-honoring. They see inconsistencies between people's words/actions and biblical teaching others overlook or may not catch. Prophets speak to the people, bringing edification, encouragement, and consolation. They warn people of the immediate or future consequences of continuing their current course of action. Sometimes we perceive that prophets bring a message of doom and gloom. In reality, prophets speak a message of challenge for wrong direction or action, yet always end with a message of hope and restoration if the message is heeded.

Distinguishing of Spirits is about conviction.

Adjectives that may describe a person with the gift of Distinguishing of Spirits are:

Confronting	Convicting	Uncompromising
Penetrating	Outspoken	Authentic
	Compelling	

Teaching

Greek: didaskalia = instruction, the act of imparting the truth

The divine ability to understand and clearly explain God's truths, and to show how we can apply these in our lives. People with this gift enjoy studying the Bible and inspire listeners to greater obedience to God's word. They prepare through study and reflection and pay close attention to detail. In addition to communicating facts, they are careful to show that the Scriptures have practical applications. They can adapt their presentation in order to communicate God's message to a particular audience effectively.

Teaching is about application.

Adjectives that may describe a person with the gift of Teaching are:

Articulate	Analytical	Practical
Well-grounded	Authoritative	Incisive
	Teachable	

Message of Wisdom

Greek: logos = something said, utterance, communication
sophia = wisdom, higher or lower, earthly or spiritual

The God-given ability to understand and apply biblical and spiritual knowledge to complex, contradictory, or other difficult situations. People with the gift of Message of Wisdom have an ability to understand and live God's will. They share their wisdom with others through teaching and admonition. As with the gift of Message of Knowledge, the term "message of wisdom" is intentional. The wisdom is not for one's own benefit, but must be shared. People with this gift speak God's truth as found in Scripture, in order to provide clarity and direction to people who are struggling with which way they should go. They make practical application of biblical truths. They are, in effect, a "compass" for the body of Christ.

Message of Wisdom is about guidance.

Adjectives that may describe a person with the gift of Message of Wisdom are:

Reasonable	Thoughtful	Clear-sighted
Skillful	Obedient to God's Will	Sensible

The following three gifts are self-evident, charismatic gifts of the Spirit that point to God and/or are signs of God's power.

Speaking in Tongues

Greek: *glōssa* = tongues, a language, specifically one not naturally learned

The divine ability to speak a message from God to the people in a language one has not naturally learned. The gift of tongues is a sign to unbelievers showing the power and glory of God. There seem to be three types of tongues: speaking in a language the speaker does not know, but the listener does; speaking in a language neither the speaker nor the listeners understand, which requires an interpreter; and a private prayer language. The first two build up the body of Christ. The third edifies the speaker and is used in private prayer to commune with God.

Interpretation of Tongues

Greek: *hermēneia* = translation
***glōssa* = tongues, a language, specifically one not naturally learned**

The divine ability to translate the message of someone speaking in tongues. People who use this gift may or may not also have the gift of speaking in tongues, and they may or may not remember the message they interpret when they have finished doing so. People with this gift enable the gift of tongues to build up the church, by interpreting God's message for the people.

Miraculous Powers

Greek: energēma = an effect, working, operation
dynamis = force, power, specifically miraculous power

The divine ability to perform miracles that testify to the truth of the gospel. People with this gift perform miracles (also referred to as "signs" and "wonders") among the people for the purpose of getting their attention, so as to point to the mighty works of God, testifying to the truth of the gospel in order to lead people to faith. The performance of these miracles leads to listening, following, and believing in the message by those who witness them.